The inner ramblings of a mad man

George Hawkes

BookLeaf Publishing

Presentation by *BookLeaf Publishing*

Web: www.bookleafpub.com

E-mail: info@bookleafpub.com

ISBN: 9789357211727

First edition 2023

DEDICATION

This book is dedicated to those who are in a struggle just know it does get easier.

This book is also dedicated to my beloved son Logan, i am proud of you everyday

ACKNOWLEDGEMENT

I'd, like to thank my close friend Kat, for being the push i needed to pull my finger out and get this done.

I'd also like to thank all of those who have supported me through the best of times and the worst of times

PREFACE

For all intense and purposes I decided to write a book, there is no one poem that is relevant however a few poems may interlink and that is all part of my design, I initially started this as a way of dealing with my depression and anxiety adding bits to it over the years, some of the material you are about to read may trigger some readers, I never intended for this to see the light of day and the title is rather fitting.
So get a cup of tea, or your choice of beverage and sit back and welcome to the inner ramblings of my mind.

Midnight confession

I'm just so done with people using me and backstabbing me, I'm not perfect and I don't claim to be I have my flaws maybe one too many but I'm a human being, I'm up and I'm down life isn't a rollercoaster it's being stranded at sea and drowning but not dying, this pressure is immense and it keeps getting harder it's useless, it's hopeless its never ending

Why do we love ?

The hardest thing to do is to be honest with a girl

This is multiplied when you love her

You give them your heart on a plate they stab it
with there claws and make you swell with hate.

He was right falling in love is easy but falling
out of love takes a bit of practice.

My heart is open on the floor bleeding like it has
done many times before you say in a couple
days ill change my mind but I've know for a
while I want to call you mine.

But its fine for this I'll publish at my own
request I'll slit my wrists and hope for the best
don't mourn for me but never forget my undying
love for you will not rest.

Cowardly courageous

Beyond the recess of space and time
There is something in my mind
Like tequila shots with out the lime
I know that love is hard to find

Maybe its true its better to have loved and lost
then to ever have loved at all
Just grab the girl ask her out who cares if you
look a fool

Her poem

If I had the chance to make you smile for you
my dear I'd walk a thousand miles

With no shoes no socks across hot sand until my
feet are chapped and callused like my hands

For with you in my life everything is bright even
on these cold and dark winter nights

But all I ask is a chance and hope you don't over
glance the fact we have a chemistry and I know
it can't just be me

I'd hold your hand like I have done before and
keep you safe until the crack of dawn for you are
the one I've been waiting for

I've made some mistakes in my life I know I'm
not perfect but I do try

But for you I'd bleed myself dry

Demons

There are demons in all of us some of us can repel then better than others where as people like me our demons run a muck and take control and hurt the people we love so this it my confession.

Bleak and better understanding of myself

The twisted reality behind my insanity isn't just a trait I long to forget.
A disaster can be averted if you take time with everything and just take a step back and listen
The way I feel cannot be comprehended nor can I put it in words this place I'm in is cancerous and life draining there is no end to the means of this.
Underappreciated and overwhelmed as I scream bloody murder just to find away out of this self compromising and leaving my mask broken im left to say was it worth it, the answer I don't know

Please

Nothing else matters when you're at the top
The man who has everything but nothing at the same time
Yes I may have a child and I may have a job, a roof over my head , clothes on my back
But that doesn't stop my mind from telling me to do unspeakable things
To grab the razors and make myself pay
Each day is a battle in this never ending war
Please with the quickest of ease tell me im worth it
Tell me you're proud
Please can someone love me
I really don't have much else

Why

Why am I like this
Why do I hurt
Why do I get attached
Why surely I must be cursed
Why am I still trying
Why do I care
Why haven’t I picked up the razor blade
Why haven’t I cut my myself
Why its the sign of growing
Why its the sign of strength
Why did I love another
Why don’t I love myself
Why do these voices mock me
Why do they scream so loud
Why can’t I just hold one last time
Why is it so wrong
Why is the mood changing
Why would you want to be my friend
Why is everything so fucked up
Why are the tears coming from your face
Why is it I am broken
Why is suicide my destined fate

When friends become lovers

It can be awkward at first learning each others
likes and dislikes
But when your puzzle pieces, everything just
seems right
Not matter what happens between them they
know that they have friends that will stand by
them in the last garrison
Although their love may seem quite random, a
welcome surprise despite personal suspicion
They go together as if life intended it, not a
stupid fling, and not a one night incident,
brewing over time, whether at matter of seconds,
days, years or minutes there's no denying a
chemical reaction
Oxygen and nitrogen together is what I need
their loving atmosphere is the air I breathe

It was on my mind

Someone save me from myself, realse me from my mental health, a breakdown silenced by the masses all alone and soon to be in wooden caskets.

She made me feel this way

I feel warm and I feel fuzzy
I feel scared and excited
I don’t recall the last time I felt this way
I don't feel dead inside I don't feel like cutting
I feel alive and full of purpose and for the first
time I actually deserve it
Its a funny thing to be like this so happy when
im use to feeling shit
Nothing is quite like this feeling when all you've
had is bad luck
Its something that feel and I feel it in my gut
It makes my tummy rumble just like butterflies
It leads me to the answer that is
Im in
Love

Broken

The mind is like a vase
You knock it over and it breaks
Its hard to fix and the glue never sticks.

A broken mind leads to a broken person a broken person doesn't know how to love or even what love is, however these broken people aren't a rare occurrence they just hide in plain sight. They've been hurt one to many times abused physically and mentally and sometimes sexually to the point they have exploded into tiny pieces. Once in a while someone comes along and picks up your pieces and helps you rebuild upon a once previous flawed design making you feel invincible you develop trust and feel normal

Conflicted

I don't know how to say this
I don't know what words to use
My feelings for you have never left me
Even after how I was used
You still mean everything to me
Even if you'll never be mine
I don't want us to have boundaries
And I don't want to lie
But when I said I loved you
For the very first time
I meant every syllable
Every consonant and every vowel
Even after all this time
Your name is the one I want to howl

The queen and her jester

I'm not a brave knight and I don't ride a noble stead
I don't wear heavy armour, chainmail or drink mead
I'm your court jester with bells on my hat, taking the piss out of everyone, most importantly myself
You are a beautiful and flawless woman, a queen by all accounts
Queens marry princes or knights and not the jester who make the laugh at night
For a jester is all I am
I'm not the strongest, or most handsome kind of man
I don't carry a sword or shield but I do look good in tights
But for you my queen I shall hold out a burning light,
as I lay down my jesters hat and learn how to fight
For although I am a jester
I have many tricks up my sleeve, but if my confession falters and I fall off of my stolen stead

And should our enemies find me and they will certainly make me bleed
my love you my fair maiden will save me in the end
For a jesters job isn't to defend

When I see her

When I see her my heart it flutters
When I see her my words they stutter
When I see her everything feels right
When I see her I have second sight
When I see her she makes me feel alright
But regardless of what I want
Regardless of what I desire
Ill be a friend in her eyes, never get to show her
what I have to offer, my age a permanent
blunder, a toy boy maybe
But I could be her one and only life time lover.

Fixation

A constant fixation in my mind, her body is perfect and her eyes are mysterious and magical. This hypnotic spell im under is the constant realization of my lack of concentration, A reflection on my newly appointed declaration, throwing away my own personal desolation, there she stands my revelation in the light and shining aura of my soul, the reason for my recent over masturbation and heavy ejaculation, for she truly is my biggest fascination, my love for her is the only destination I plan to vacation. For I may be lovesick and there's only one form of vaccination for my for my addiction, A kiss, long and passionate to seal the deal
And there you have it, my new fixation, the real reason behind my pupils dilation, maybe im crazy or I just need an outsiders observation, to give me conformation and the information I need to court my future companion, my partner in crime.

Desolation and Agony

Now this isn't a confession or a suicide note this is how I feel and how I'm choosing to emote I'm not the smartest man nor am I the best I'm not attractive and don't have loads of friends.
People come to me to unburden there sins and confessions but now asks how I am or how I'm holding up I'm tired of these people taking my advice but not being there when I need some in return I'm tired of just being a joke to these people I'm fed up of being their tool.
My wrists are scarred and show how I deal with my problems how I deal with the desolation and depression I'm bestowed, I don't cut myself for attention or steal your girls affection. I self harm and mutilate my body, I'm an artist and my canvas is my skin my brushes are razor blades and my blood is the paint

Lost in love

Lost in her eyes that shine like diamonds in the
Night's sky
There's no other place id rather be than between
her thighs
Im not going to lie, but if my heart she should
deny I think id break down and cry
Maybe a bit melodramatic but I would probably
die
Because when things feel right its like sparks
and the chemistry is undeniable
I hope she realises that I am more than just a
young man, im hopelessly devoted
To the point I'm going to show this.
Show this, a collection of words with
interlinking themes to some the subject matter
maybe
Obscene.
My body aches for her touch but I play a game
where im teased, as she knows what im capable
of.
The thing is, this isn't just about the sex, its
everything.
For she is everything I've ever needed

She silences my demons

There are many things I know for certain, the
sun will set at dusk and rise at first dawn, I know
the early bird catches the worm, and the grass
isn't always greener.
I don't claim to have all the answers and im
certainly not the smartest
But a smile like yours shines the brightest,
brighter than the sun, you don't understand how
special you really are to me
When im with you, My thoughts are at ease, I
don't feel angry, I feel at peace.
When I look at you not only do I see angels but
you
Silence my demons

Hopeless no more

I used to be hopelessly devoted to the motion of true love, but its not until you discover its a lie you begin to trust and become someone else. There is hope for the hopeless and no matter the amount of romantic notions or potions can change the biological location of their heart, its better to have loved then lost than to have ever loved at all if that's too cliché then let me restart. A closing message for those in need, be who you can be, don't become someone you aren't comfy with living your life a lie is not a substitute for not being able to live your life the way you want too, who cares if you're over or underweight, whether the commotion of your self promotion gathers you unwanted attention, be you for who you are and please don't go changing just to please

The Dangers of love

Looking at me with those beautiful eyes preying
upon me like a tiger in the wild
She doesn't know how just how adorable, how
cute and how perfect she is
Her body is a landscape and im going to explore
it from head to toe and every crevice in between
I wish she could see im the one she needs, not
the other jokers appearing out of greed
Their gluttony is appalling when they have what
I want at home.
But this a poem I have written for you to never
see, I know you'll never reciprocate the same
feeling for me
I know now the dangers of love

www.ingramcontent.com/pod-product-compliance
Lightning Source LLC
Chambersburg PA
CBHW051759130826
49812CB00033B/1202
* 9 7 8 9 3 5 7 2 1 1 7 2 7 *